Self-Leadership Guide

SELF-LEADERSHIP GUIDE

Be empowered and be motivated

By

Peter Khoury

SELF-LEADERSHIP GUIDE FIRST EDITION 2011

The Self-Leadership Guide is available at special discounts when purchased in bulk for premiums and sales promotions, as well as for fund-raising or educational use. Special editions or excerpts can also be created to specification. For details, contact the author.

Book designed by Whim Design Place, LLC.
www.whimdesignplace.com
510-931-7768

www.SelfLeadershipGuide.com
San Francisco, CA 94107
ISBN 978-0-9838257-0-8
Printed in the United States of America
Published simultaneously in Canada
Red Crow Publishing

This book is dedicated to the greatest power in you, the power to self-lead and create your own future.

Most of all, to my parents, to my brothers, to my friends, and to my wife.

Contents

Acknowledgment ix

Preface x - xii

INTRODUCTION

Self-Leadership and the Future of Work 13 - 17

PHASE I: PREPARE YOUR MIND

How to Use this Book: Step-by-Step Instructions 18 - 19

Centering Exercise: Get Calm and Focused 20 - 21

Self-Assessment: Determine Where You Stand 22 - 26

What Is Your Job IQ? 27 - 28

PHASE II: DISCOVERING YOUR SELF-LEADERSHIP CODE

Steps to Discovering Your Self-Leadership Code 29

The Power of Knowing Your Code 30 - 32

List of Things that Are Most Important to You in a Job 33 - 35

Six Things that Are Most Important to You in a Job 36 - 37

Transform the Negative into the Positive and Win 38 - 39

The Power of Knowing What You Want 40 - 43

Your Six Most Important Job Requirements: Ultra Focus 44 - 45

The Power of Simplicity 46 - 47

Sequence Your Career Code: Prioritize Your Six Most Important
Job Requirements 48 - 55

Working Consciously with Your Poweful Unconscious 56 - 58

PHASE III: YOUR SELF-LEADERSHIP CODE IN ACTION:

Match Your Job Requirements, Your Career Code, with Concrete
Projects and Activities 59 - 62

The SMART Goals System: A Tool for Setting and Achieving
Goals 63 - 72

Taking Action to Job Satisfaction! 73 - 77

Contents

Your Current Job and Your Code: Does Your Current Job Honor Your Career Code? Are Your Most Important Job Requirements Being Met in Your Current Job? 78 - 82

Three Stategies to Achieve Fulfillment and Empowerment at Work: What to do when Your Most Important Job Requirements Are Not Being Fulfilled in Your Current Job 83 - 88

Talking Your Way to Success and Satisfaction: Sharpen Your Communication Skills 89 - 94

The Nex Step: Be the Ultimate Leader: Lead by the Code! 95 - 98

CONCLUSION: YOUR ARE NOT A LOBSTER 99 - 101

RESOURCE GUIDE 102 - 105

ABOUT PETER KHOURY 106

CUSTOM RESOURCE 107 - 108

EXTRA WORKSHEETS 109

Acknowledgments

Thanks to the many people who spent hours reading, reviewing and giving feedback on the initial drafts of this book. There are too many of you to mention, but you will find your influence throughout these pages.

I want to give special thanks to Gery Pappa, a great reader and implementer; Dr. Thomas Voris for his feedback and input; Joumana Zeid, my wife, for great support, feedback and alignment on this project; Zorica Gojkovic, my editor and coach, for making this a reality; and Alan Ovson for being a great mentor and ally.

Most of all, I want to thank my clients, who always challenged themselves and had the courage to look inside for what is possible and to achieve it. They have inspired me over the years and have made this book possible.

Preface

"Self-leadership is knowing what you want and going for it."

This book came about because of my search for a fulfilling, motivating, and, at the same time, financially rewarding career. In this book, I reveal the tools that I discovered on my journey to career fulfillment and empowerment. I went from being unhappy with my job to being excited and motivated to wake up every single day and do the work that I do. Below is my story and thus the story of the book.

Five years ago, I had, by everyone's standards, a good pharmaceutical engineering job, yet I was miserable. The job paid well, I had a fancy title, and I even got to lead people and projects, but I woke up every day dreading to go to work.

To help myself get through this, I read self-help books. I said the affirmations and tried to be positive. However, nothing worked. I went to work every day, put a smile on my face, and did a great job. At the end of the day, I drove home worn out. All I knew was that this was not normal. I deserved to be happy at work.

Though the bonuses, the raises, and the promotions acted as a temporary relief, soon their effects wore off and I became miserable again.

I went back to school to get my MBA and even started my own convenience store business. Yet, just like the bonuses and raises, the school and the business turned out to be short-term solutions. Soon afterwards, the temporary relief was gone and I felt miserable again.

At that point, I knew that I was stuck and that I needed help. A friend of mine recommended that I see a life coach. At that time, I had no idea what a life coach was, but I was desperate enough to try anything. I did some research and finally hired someone.

Working with the coach, I started to understand what I wanted and how to get it. The coach introduced me to the concept of self-leadership. He showed me how to identify what motivates me and how to go after it strategically.

My big realization was that, to be happy, I needed to work with people instead of computers. I also needed to do creative work, which was not part of my pharmaceutical job. This led me to the realization that I wanted to be a coach and a professional speaker instead of an engineer and a storeowner.

After that, I decided to quit my pharmaceutical engineering job, sell my convenience store, and pursue the coaching career that satisfied my passions.

The past five years have been magical, fulfilling, and financially rewarding. I have to admit that there were a few hiccups here and there, but my motivation, energy, and happiness never wavered.

If you are not happy, motivated, and excited with what you are doing, then read this book and do the exercises, and you too will be on your way to enjoying your career. Now is the time to be motivated and empowered at work. Do not delay. Do not put off your own happiness.

Do not worry though; you might not have to leave your current job as I did. Sometimes, there are treasures under our feet and we are not aware of them. With the empowering tools in this book, you might be able to get what you want in your current position and industry. Follow the process and you will know what to do at the end.

I intend to guide you through a process similar to the one I went through with my coach, and that I now use with my coaching clients. I have modified and refined the process over the years and present it to you in this book in its most effective form.

I have written this book because help of this sort is not out there, though it's very much needed. People always asked me for book recommendations and I could not find anything that would truly help them. In this book, I've refined the exercises I use in my private sessions so that you can get the same benefit as you would if you were working with me directly.

Over the years, with my training, writing, and coaching sessions, I have helped hundreds of people obtain exciting careers. I've helped my clients find themselves, figure out what they wanted, and then get it.

Now, with this book, you can have the same success. With a little work and effort, you, too, can have fulfillment in your chosen work and enhanced happiness in your life.

Self-Leadership and the Future of Work

"It matters not how strait the gate,
How charged with punishments the scroll,
I am the master of my fate:
I am the captain of my soul."
William Ernest Henley

This book is based on three fundamental tenets: One, working for a paycheck alone does not make you happy at work. Two, you have more power than you realize over your situation at work. Three, with self-leadership tools, you can be instrumental in bringing about your own success and happiness at work.

Professionals from every walk of life–from different generations, different socioeconomic backgrounds, and different cultures–recognize that work is more than just about the paycheck. These professionals are no longer content with clocking in, doing the work, and clocking out. Instead, they want work tailored to their specific needs. They are not accepting their fate in an organization, but are finding ways to break the mold. They seek to contribute to the well-being of the organization, while, at the same time, doing work that inspires them. These professionals are what I call enlightened rebels or self-leaders.

Self-leadership is an enlightened rebellion. The rebellion part is about individuality and non-conformity. The enlightened part is about keeping the well-being of the organization in mind.

With the proper tools, self-leaders can serve the goals of their organization and simultaneously achieve their own personal goals and visions. Furthermore, a self-leader's success and happiness are not limited by and do not depend on his or her manager's ability. Certainly, having a good manager helps, but it is not essential to achieving fulfillment at work.

Self-leadership means taking charge of the self. It is the prerequisite to all forms of leadership. After all, if a person can't lead himself or herself, can't be self-determining, how can he or she lead others?

> **"True leadership starts with self-leadership."**

Self-leaders want happiness, success, and meaningful work. They no longer accept the status quo. CEOs, managers, supervisors, and employees are becoming enlightened rebels by discovering, celebrating, and expressing their uniqueness at work through projects that are tailored to their specific needs and wants, yet that are aligned with the organization's vision and mission.

The work world as we know it today has been shaped by multiple revolutions: the agricultural revolution, the industrial revolution, and the information revolution.

But although revolutions have their purpose in shaping history and humanity as a whole, there is no inherent guarantee in them to make you personally happy.

What is taking place today is a rebellion led by self-leaders. A rebellion is individualistic and independent. A revolution is dominated by the movement of the masses.

A revolution is lead by group desire; a rebellion is lead by individualistic desire. To guarantee personal happiness and satisfaction, you need enlightened rebellion. You need self-leadership.

Individuals in different organizations start by leading themselves to move things forward and to be happy. Professionals in every field of endeavor can choose to carve their own paths every single day. They no longer have to be helpless objects in the nine-to-five machinery. They are rebels and they are individuals; they are the creators of their own destiny, the captains of their souls.

Revolutions have been great at causing massive changes in the world, changes on a macro scale. The big changes revolutions bring may or may not help you. On the other hand, with rebellion, you are causing micro changes that affect you directly and that have a direct impact on your life and happiness.

Being a rebel is hard because the rebel's path is the path less traveled. Yet this is the path that is the most rewarding. A rebel at work does not listen to the masses, is not influenced by peer pressure, and only listens to his or her heart.

The enlightened rebel at work is a modern-day hero who is not afraid to follow his or her calling, do what he or she loves to do, and make a great living doing it.

The workplace of today is full of enlightened rebels. Maybe you are one of them. Maybe you want to become one! This book is for you.

You no longer need to just follow the masses, do whatever you are told to do, and hope that one day you can be happy and fulfilled at work. You can be happy and fulfilled right now with whatever you are doing. The tools in this book will show you how.

There is some work involved and some soul searching required. Most importantly, you have to be open to hear your calling. The calling is always there, you just have to listen. The exercises in this book will help you open your ears and heart to get you ready for a fulfilling, rewarding, and extraordinary future no matter where you are on the career ladder.

Most jobs can be fulfilling and rewarding for the person who knows what he or she wants. For those who don't know what they want, no job in the universe will do.

To be a rebel, first you have to find out what it is that you want, which is currently not being fulfilled at work. Then you have to do everything in your power to satisfy that which is missing.

The act of taking control of your happiness at work is rebellious in nature. You don't have to wait for things to change, for your superiors to figure it out, for things to fix themselves. Just take an active roll and make things happen. That is self-leadership.

Now, for the first time in history, work is no longer about just making a living. Work is about being more and doing more of what you want. It is about expressing yourself and pursuing whatever you want and need. We are no longer bound by some arbitrary standard or by the limitations of the era in which we live. We are free to have whatever we want and still make a living at it. All we have to do is find out what we want, what is important to us, what makes us unique in our search for fulfilling work, and then go after it.

As you read this book, you might wonder if it's possible to have all you want in a job and still contribute to the growth and harmony of your organization. The answer is YES!

In fact, if everyone knew exactly what they wanted and went for it, we would have less conflict, less friction, more productivity, and more collaboration.

This book will help you clarify exactly what it is that you want. Furthermore, it will open your eyes to the fact that most people want different things than you do. This realization will lead to a better understanding of yourself and others and will help you develop win/win outcomes for everyone involved. For this is the way of the self-leader at work, to consistently create win/win situations.

This book is a guide to your career direction, satisfaction, and success. We all lose our way, lack motivation, and feel confused at different points in our careers. It happens to the best of us and there is nothing wrong with that unless we surrender, give up, and allow it to affect our happiness and performance. The most successful professionals I know have a way to get back on track, find their direction again, and gain the motivation to move forward and get what they want.

Here is a big promise for you: *At the end of this book, you will have a way to know what makes you excited and motivated at work and you will know exactly how to get it.*

You will be focused, clear, and moving in the right direction. If you think you are doing well with your career now, this book will take you to the next level and will fine-tune your success and satisfaction even more.

Let me tell you what this book is *not*:

This is *not* a theory book. This is not a résumé-writing book. This is not a hype and motivation book. This book is not meant to be an intellectual exercise. There are millions of such books in the market today. This book is different.

This is a hands-on career-coaching guide. You will get the feeling that you're sitting with me in my office getting high-value coaching sessions. Step by step, I will show you what makes you tick and what motivates you. I will explain to you what you most want and help you get it. You and I will work through this process together; we will be partners.

This is a process that I've used with hundreds of satisfied clients in one-on-one sessions and in seminars. This does not mean that it will be easy. You might be challenged, hesitant, and frustrated at times. All I ask of you is to stick with the process and you will be rewarded with increased clarity, focus, and motivation at the end. You will get excited about work again.

PHASE I : PREPARE YOUR MIND

How to Use this Book: Step-by-Step Instructions

To get the most out of this book, follow these simple recommendations.

1. Use pen and paper.

This book is not meant for passive reading. Take notes, do the exercises, and write down your findings, thoughts, and insights. Use your own journal or the downloadable workbook [www.SelfLeadershipGuide. com].

2. Find a quiet place where you will not be disturbed for a little while.

You will need to do some reflecting on one of the most important parts of your life. Invest some quiet time to think clearly and completely. It will be worth it.

3. Do the centering exercise before you start or resume working with this book.

Stress, fear, worry, and anxiety can lead to bad decisions. It's important to work with this book with a clear head and an open heart. To help you get into a powerful and productive state, I've provided a simple and quick exercise that you can do regularly before you start working with this book.

4. Do the exercises in this book in fifteen-minute chunks.

It's important to take regular breaks to allow time for rest and reflection. Take time to reflect on the insights you have gained.

5. Give and receive feedback.

If something is not clear, go to www.SelfLeadershipGuide.com, ask your question, and get supportive material. You will gain tremendously from sharing your insights and from reading what others share.

6. Work through to the end of the book.

99.9% of people never finish the books they buy. This book is small and easy to read. For maximum results, make sure you finish it completely without skipping any sections. Also, don't be surprised if you feel the need to come back to the book again and again for further insights as you move forward.

7. Have fun!

Gem mining is fun for many people because occasionally they find an expensive precious stone in the rough. I encourage you to do the exercises in this book with the same anticipation and excitement as a miner, and you too will keep discovering precious gems of insight that could change your life and work forever.

PHASE I : PREPARE YOUR MIND
Centering Exercise: Get Calm and Focused

In order to learn about yourself, you will have to go beyond the surface chatter of your mind. You will have to access a deeper part of yourself. If you stay on the surface, you will be distracted by all the noise and interference and will miss the truth of who you are.

In case you didn't already know, in a larger reality, you are not your fear, stress, anxiety, frustration, confusion, or any other negative or even positive emotion you may feel. You are much more.

To access this deeper side of you, the side of you beyond your emotions, you need to put aside the surface chatter and the daily distractions, and focus on your intrinsic self.

The following exercise will put you in an expansive and focused state to help you access your center.

Fortunately, you don't have to meditate for years to achieve this state. This simple centering exercise will help you remember and experience inner well-being so you can get the most out of this book.

Read the bullets below and follow the instructions before you start or resume working with this book. After doing the centering exercise several times, you will be able to access the desired open and centered state without reading the directions any more. Until then, feel free to go through the complete exercise by coming back to this page any time you need to.

- Start here
- As you sit and read these lines, pay closer attention to the shapes of the   letters on this page. Direct your attention towards the seat in which you are sitting. Feel it underneath you and how hard or soft it is on your body.
- Now, pay attention to how your body is responding to the chair. Feel your body resting on the chair. Feel your hands, feel your feet , and take a deep breath.
- Notice your breathing as you read on.
- Notice your thoughts and let them be. Just notice. Be the observer and nothing more.
- While reading, notice things in your peripheral vision without moving your head or eyes, things to which you haven't been paying attention before.   Notice them as you expand your vision; let them in and breathe.
- Expand your hearing. Notice the sounds around you. What sounds can you hear?
- Feel your clothes on your body. Feel the temperature of your skin. Get a sense of how you feel inside now.
- Things around you might feel calmer; you might feel quieter and more centered.
- Remember this feeling as you read and re-read this exercise and the rest of this book. Try to maintain this level of Centeredness while you are going through life.
- Now breathe some more.

Remember, you can come back to this exercise any time you like. Doing this exercise before you continue reading will put you in an open state where you feel completely yourself. Your new awareness will give you more accurate results when you do the other exercises in this book.

PHASE I : PREPARE YOUR MIND
Self-Assessment: Determine Where You Stand

"Before you go anywhere, you have to know where you are."

Before you go anywhere with your career, you need to know where you currently stand. It's like using Google Maps. You have to enter your current location and your destination. Without knowing where you are, there is no way you can get directions to where you want to go. The same thing applies to your career. Where you start determines how you will get where you want to be.

Below are a few questions that will help you identify where you are right now with your job or career.

To start, first answer the questions below by replying Yes or No. When you are done, go back to the questions where your answer was Yes and read the explanation below the question. This will tell you how this book can help you.

Once done, proceed to the career IQ test.

_____ Do you feel that something is missing in your current job?

You might like some things about your current job–maybe the technical challenge, maybe the industry, or maybe the people you work with–but something might feel missing. You can't put your finger on it, but you know that something is not there. It's annoying at first, but, little by little, it becomes a thorn in your side. The thorn drains your energy and motivation.

You can spend your whole career wondering what is missing. But it does not have to be this way. In this book, you will find out what is missing and will learn how to fix it. This will make you feel more complete, more satisfied, and happier at work.

_____ Are you working in a job that does not inspire you?

Your job was exciting at first, but not anymore. If you are bored at your job, if you have lost the excitement and inspiration, you need to tap into the source of excitement again. If you don't do this, it will cost you in productivity, success, and motivation in the long run. There is nothing worse than going to work uninspired. You just clock in and wait for the day to be over.

It does not have to be this way; your work could be exciting and inspiring. When you are inspired and excited, the time will start to fly. You won't be waiting desperately for the shift to be over. Imagine the energy you would go home with after a great day at work.

This book will show you how to connect to your source of motivation at your current or future job.

_____ Do you feel like you have a job, but you've lost yourself?

After working for years at a job, you might notice that you have lost yourself. You are disconnected from your values, identity, strengths, and source of power. You go through the motions every day, but you feel that the job is taking you away from your soul. It's robbing you of your true identity.

The perfect job for you is the one that is aligned with your true identity, who you truly are. It will help you grow professionally and personally.

This book will help you connect with who you really are and what you really want.

_____ Are you at a loss as to what you want in a career?

Sometimes it's hard to see the trees from the forest when it comes to our careers. You may feel lost, confused, and disillusioned. What you actually do in your job is nothing like what you anticipated; it's not what you signed up for. You had different expectations and now you have to live with what you got. You know you want something different, but you don't know where to go and what to do.

This book will give you the clarity you need to make the right career moves. The insight and direction you get will help you decide intelligently how best to go forward. The decisions you make will not be haphazard; they will be part of a set of logical choices to get you moving in the direction that is right for you. This will ensure that you don't end up in the same position ever again.

_____ Can't make a decision about a career?

You are a person who wants to do it all. You know and are good at many things. You probably have a long list of things you want to do. You want to be an artist, an architect, an engineer, and an entrepreneur. Each of these jobs is important to you because it fulfills a deep need.

This book will help you leverage your abilities so you can focus on one of the things you want to do, succeed at it, and, at the same time, satisfy all your other needs.

_____ Do you have a hard time with your manager or colleagues?

If you have conflict with management or other professionals, if you have issues with the politics of it all, and if people in your organization push your buttons, this book will give you insights as to why this is happening and the tools to handle this challenge.

We all want different things from work. You will get a clear understanding of what you want and why you want it. With this clarity, you can ask for and get what you desire.

In addition, going through this process will increase your appreciation for what others want and expect out of work. Your newfound understanding of these differences will help you empathize with the people around you so that you can resolve conflict more quickly.

_____ Do you want advanced leadership skills for this new economy?

The economy has changed. We have different demographics in the workplace and a different type of worker. The old ways of leading no longer work. A new, innovative leadership approach is required.

In the past, people who worked in a company or department usually came from the same town, the same schools, and the same community. These days, that's not the case. People working with you come from different cultures, different schools, different economic backgrounds, different generations, and different sets of values and beliefs. They all want different things from their careers. There is no more a "one shoe fits all" kind of leadership.

Leadership starts with self-leadership. Once you understand how to lead yourself to career success and fulfillment, you will be able to lead others.

In this book, you will get the tools to understand yourself and what makes you different. In turn, the insights you gain about yourself will help you understand how others are different.

_____ Do you want to understand today's work culture?

In addition to all the socioeconomic and demographic changes in the workplace, we also have a new type of professional. Say hello to the "knowledge worker."

The "knowledge worker" is a term coined by Peter Drucker in the early '50s to describe a new type of professional in an organization. This type of worker does most of his or her work in his or her head.

In the past, when Drucker invented the term, most of the workers in the United States were industrial workers or those who performed manual labor. Things have changed. Since the early '90s, the knowledge worker has dominated the work place.

The leadership tools that existed in the past worked for leading the industrial worker. They don't work for the knowledge worker.

In this book, you will get the latest tools to lead yourself to success as a knowledge worker. Once you master these tools, you might find yourself naturally applying them to others around you and thus becoming a leader.

_____ Do you want to change your career, but don't know in which direction to go?

You are at a point where you want to change your career. You are either retiring from a long career or changing careers because you are unhappy with what you are doing. You want something new and exciting. This book will save you time and effort by helping you zero in on what you want and giving you the tools to get it. It will point you in the right direction so your next job is exactly what you want it to be.

Whoever you are and whatever your situation, this book will move you toward career fulfillment and an all-around happier life.

PHASE I : PREPARE YOUR MIND
What Is Your Job IQ?

Clients often ask me to give them career assessments. To help them, I've developed this quick audit. It will accurately predict your potential for happiness and success in your current job or career. It will give you a clear picture of where you are right now and where you are heading. The rest of this book will give you tools to make corrections to your path so that you land somewhere you love.

Directions:

Rate yourself in each area on a scale of 0-10 (0 = not true, 10 = very true). When you are done, add up the points.

You are happy with your current career direction.	_____
You are happy with what you do.	_____
You are motivated at work.	_____
Your job is aligned with your career ambitions.	_____
You have clear job and career goals.	_____
Your job and career goals are motivating and inspiring.	_____
You know what is important to you in your job.	_____
Your current job honors your values.	_____
You feel that you have both happiness and financial success in your chosen career.	_____
You know exactly what you want from your current job.	_____
Total Career IQ Score	_____

Your Results:

If your career IQ score is 75 and above: You are doing well with your career choices. You are making very intelligent decisions about your future and happiness. Based on your score, your career potential is high. This book will give you further insights and will help you optimize your career choices even more.

If your career IQ score is between 55 and 75: You are doing okay with your career choices. Your decisions are not optimal, and they are not aligned. You might have conflicting desires and goals, or maybe you are not congruent with your true values and identity. Based on your score, your career potential for success and happiness needs some adjustment. This book will change all that for you. It will help you become more congruent and clearer about what you want, and will help you set more empowering goals.

If your career IQ score is below 55: You really need this book. You can be happy, motivated, have aligned goals, and have a great career that will financially and emotionally reward you. I know hundreds of people who are doing it and if you start looking carefully, you will see them all around you.

Based on your score, your career potential for success and happiness needs some work. This book will start you in the right direction and raise your career IQ dramatically so you can find success and happiness in your chosen career. No worries, though, I will coach you through the process, and at the end you will feel a remarkable difference.

In Addition:

The score you get is just an estimation of where you are. There is nothing wrong or right about it. From my experience, people who score high tend to have smoother, happier, and more successful careers than those who score low. That's why it can be a predictor of your career potential. If you have a low score, you are missing fundamental elements in your career development. This book will help you fill in the gaps easily and build a stronger career foundation fast.

So turn the page and let's take the first step to your unprecedented career satisfaction.

PHASE II: DISCOVERING YOUR SELF-LEADERSHIP CODE
Steps to Discovering Your Self-Leadership Code

"Work is love made visible."
From The Prophet, by Kahlil Gibran

You want more than a paycheck. Although money is important, you need many more things from your job to make you happy, successful, and productive. The specific set of requirements that you need to be happy in a job is what I call your *self-leadership code, or the code.* An example of some requirements might be freedom, ethics, integrity, a fast-paced environment, etc. Your self-leadership code is unique. Everyone else will have his or her own.

Armed with your code, your identified unique job requirements, you can unlock the vault of your career potential. In the vault are all the secrets that will help you map, develop, and plan a career that will bring you success, fulfillment, and happiness.

In this section, I will lead you through a process to help you determine the things that are most important to you in a job. In this way you will discover the combination to the vault of your career potential.

PHASE II: DISCOVERING YOUR SELF-LEADERSHIP CODE
The Power of Knowing Your Code

"Knowing others is intelligence; knowing yourself is true wisdom.
Mastering others is strength; mastering yourself is true power."
Unknown author

Even though every person has a unique set of requirements that comprise his or her self-leadership code, most people are unaware of them. Being unaware of them, they cannot leverage them to create satisfying and successful careers.

To feel empowered at work and clear about your career direction, you need to have access to your code. Before you do so, it's essential that you understand its importance and power.

Once you know your code, there will be no limits to what you can achieve in your career and your personal life. Your career potential will be in your hands to direct in any way you choose to whatever success you want. You will no longer be the victim of doubt, uncertainty, and random jobs. You will know what you want and how to get it.

The code gives you certainty and saves you time.

Most people spend a lifetime going from one job to another in an effort to find one that will make them happy and satisfied. They're randomly attempting to dial the perfect combination on their career vault.

If you're trying to open the career vault randomly, you are leaving your success and happiness to chance. You might find the code accidentally, if you get lucky. If you don't get lucky, you'll spend many years wondering why you can't get it right.

Knowing your code will save time wasted on trial and error.

By reading this book, you strike me as a person who does not like to gamble with his or her career and happiness, but as one who wants to gain control over his or her career and life, and derive optimum satisfaction from both.

The code simplifies your decisions. When you know your code, your career development and advancement decisions become easy, fulfilling, and intentional.

Sera, a client of mine, discovered her code and her whole career shifted from a disconnected, meaningless, boring swirl to a fulfilling, clear, and playful journey. She progressed from taking whatever project was thrown at her to choosing appropriate projects that advanced her career. She went from having a hard time making career decisions to making great career decisions easily and quickly. Instead of being lost and unmotivated, she became clear, focused, and motivated to build a great career.

The code will empower you to manage your own career. Once you know the criteria, you can manage yourself and be less dependent on your manager.

Managers try different things to direct and motivate you and usually fail because they have no idea what your code is. Once you figure out your code, you can manage yourself and even your manager. Now, that is true empowerment.

We use criteria to make all our decisions. When you buy or rent a home, you consider certain criteria to make your final choice. You might be looking for price, location, proximity to work , or what color it is.

We do this with every decision we make; yet we neglect to follow the same process when we make the most important decision in our lives, getting the right job or career.

Finding work without a code is difficult. After graduating from college, engineering students tend to look for engineering jobs, business students tend to look for business jobs, and art students tend to look for art jobs. Soon the recent graduates realize that they are not happy with their entry-level jobs and look for another job, then another; yet happiness eludes them and finally they give up and settle for the job that pays the most. Most professionals find themselves in this sad vicious cycle.

If you're one of these people, be of good cheer. Your vicious cycle is over. In a minute, we will begin to discover your career code.

At the beginning of your career, or in a bad economy, it might be a good idea to go for any job in your field, just to get your foot in the door and support yourself. However, once you get some experience, build your industry knowledge, and have some choice in the matter, getting a job based on your code should be your ultimate goal because this is the best strategy for long-term success and happiness.

Once you know your code, you will unlock success, happiness, and true wealth beyond your wildest dreams. Yes, it's possible to have happiness, success, money, and a fulfilling career. All you have to know is the combination to your career vault your self-leadership code.

Let's discover your unique self-leadership code and get you on the road to career satisfaction!

PHASE II: DISCOVERING YOUR SELF-LEADERSHIP CODE
List of Things that Are Most Important to You in a Job

"No great thing is created suddenly."
Epictetus

In the exercise below, you will make a list of all the things that are important to you in a job.

The objective of this exercise is to write with abandon. Forget what's possible and what's not. Forget the past and any opinions you might have about your limitations. Write everything and anything that comes to mind. Don't hold back. When you feel you are done, try to write a few more things.

We want to put the critical mind aside. There will be a time and a place for it to do work, but it is not in this exercise.

Your code is buried under your conscious awareness and if you don't suspend your critical mind temporarily, it will chew up anything that tries to surface before you even realize it. The best way to prevent the chewing effect from happening is to create the largest list possible without any judgment. Later on, you will get a chance to exercise judgment about what you wrote.

Remember two things when you are doing this exercise. First, don't let its simplicity mislead you. This is a cumulative process, so it's important to do every step thoroughly and build on it. Second, be patient. Sometimes the gold comes early and sometimes it comes later on your list. Just take your time and put your thoughts on paper. The results in this exercise will be the foundation for the rest of this guide.

An effective way to prime the pump is to work with a sentence stem, such as the one below. Say the sentence stem aloud each time and complete it with whatever comes to mind.

Let's get started. What is most important to you in a job?

The most important thing to me in a job is: _____

1.	13.
2.	14.
3.	15.
4.	16.
5.	17.
6.	18.
7.	19.
8.	20.
9.	21.
10.	22.
11.	23.
12.	24.

Here are some examples of what is important to people in a job:
Good pay, close to work, good manager, good team, not working in manufacturing, working with people, working alone, working on discrete projects, not being crammed in a cubicle, being able to be creative, an upbeat environment, etc.

Finished? Great! How did it feel to do this exercise? Was it liberating? Do you feel that you've finally had a chance to identify some things that are important to you?

Remember, to get what you want, you have to know what it is first, and then you have to be able to articulate it. This exercise is the first step in the direction of getting what you want.

All right. Take a little break, and when you come back, let's continue with Step 2. Remember to do the centering exercise before you start again.

PHASE II: DISCOVERING YOUR SELF-LEADERSHIP CODE
Six Things that Are Most Important to You in a Job

In this process, you will narrow down your list to your six most important job requirements.

Let's bring your critical mind back for this step.

Look at your list and notice items that are repeated, ones that can be combined, and ones that you don't really care about.

Cross out the repetitive things and the things you don't care about, and combine what can be joined on the list.

Now consider what's left on the list and choose your top six job requirements, the things that are *most important* to you. Write these down in the table below.

It is vital that you choose six items and that you narrow the list down.

From my experience and the experience of my clients, six is the magic number. If you have more than six requirements, you will have a hard time managing the code. There will be too many things to worry about, too many variables to align. On the other hand, if you have less than six, you will have less flexibility and more restrictions.

My top six job requirements are:

1.

2.

3.

4.

5.

6.

How was that? Do you feel pretty good having identified your most important job requirements? Good. It gets better, though. Let's go to the next step.

PHASE II: DISCOVERING YOUR SELF-LEADERSHIP CODE
Transform the Negative into the Positive and Win

"Energy flows where attention goes."
Ancient Huna saying

In this process, we will utilize a powerful tool. We will convert all your job requirements into actionable, achievable statements. It is this clarity that will give you the power to create what you want (more about this in a minute). We are going to accomplish this by taking each item on your list that says what you "do not want" and converting it into what you "do want."

Look at the items where you say you do not want something in a job. It's great that you know exactly what you don't want. It's a good start. Now think about what exactly you do want. This may be a little harder, but stay with it and you will get it.

Take every "do not want" statement and ask yourself: If this is not what I want, then what do I want instead?

For example, if your statement is, "It's important not to have a bad manager," convert it into what you do want by asking yourself, What do I want instead of a bad manager? Your answers might be a "fair manager," a "good manager," a "mentoring manager," etc.

Convert every "do not want" statement into a "want" statement and write it in the space below. Make sure you include your existing "want" statements.

If all your statements are framed in the positive, skip to the next step.

The six things I most want in a job are (in the positive):

1.

2.

3.

4.

5.

6.

Do you feel the power of "wanting" something? Do you feel the way it focuses you, the way it points you in the direction of action? These are positive forces moving you toward that which is important to you.

IMPORTANT RECOMMENDATION:

I recommend that you add "pay" to your list unless you don't need money for living. If you are like most of us, pay is an important factor in your life. After all, you have to pay for food, shelter, and clothing. So, to be realistic, I suggest that you add this item to the list if you don't have it there already.

Note, that you might have to drop one code from your list if you have to add pay, because I don't recommend having more than six for the reasons discussed earlier.

PHASE II: DISCOVERING YOUR SELF-LEADERSHIP CODE

The Power of Knowing What You Want

"Passion is energy. Feel the power that comes from focusing on what excites you."
Oprah Winfrey

A "Towards" or "Away-From" Approach?

When you know what you want, you move *toward* your desires. When you know what you do not want, you move *away* from your fears.

By the simple virtue of stating what you want or do not want, you take either a "toward" or "away-from" approach to doing things.

Both approaches are strategies we utilize in our lives and each works best in its suitable context. In the context of self-leadership, the towards approach proves to be the best for long-term success and motivation.

By converting your list of important items to "wants," you take a "towards" approach. Moving towards a goal makes you clearer, more specific, and more focused.

If used as a long-term strategy, moving away from things puts you in a never-ending cycle of diffusion, confusion, and chaos.

The Power of Focus

By knowing what you want, you obtain focus. Focus has power. When you are focused, you can achieve what you want faster and more efficiently.

If you go about your career running away from things, you are relying on the never-ending process of elimination. You could spend your whole career going from one job to the next and never find what you want because the choices in life are endless. If you want to find your ideal career, you need to start moving towards what you want.

The diagram to the right shows what happens when you decide to move towards what you want or away from what you don't want.

If you use the towards approach, you will keep converging to the center of the circle: the achievement of your goals and desires. You move toward an ever-increasing focus of your talents and actualization of your potential.

Towards Direction, Focus, Clarity, and Simplicity

Away From Direction, Chaos, Complexity, and Stress

If you use the away-from approach, you will keep diverging from the center of the circle: away from your goals and desires. Moving away leads to increasing confusion and non-fulfillment.

In short-term problem-solving scenarios, a moving-

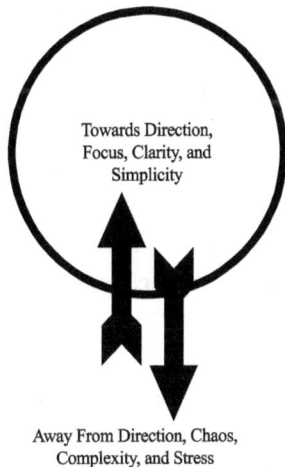

away-from strategy is sometimes useful. When you have multiple options in front of you and you have to pick one, you could use a moving-away-from strategy to eliminate the choices you like the least. This is why this strategy is used for multiple-choice tests. Your career is a long-term commitment and it's better to use the moving-towards strategy.

I once worked with a high-tech client who hated his job. When I asked him what he wanted instead of his current job, he gave me a laundry list of things he did not want. After explaining to him that listing what he did not want would not get him what he did want, but would only lead to more confusion, chaos, and frustration in his career, he thought for a second and then said that he wanted to be his own boss. "Voilà!" I said, "Now we can actually get somewhere."

Because he declared what he wanted, we were able to set specific goals, milestones, and a plan for him to transition out of his current job. Six months after our initial appointment, he left his job and started his own T-shirt printing company and had two corporate clients in contract with him. This illustrates the power of going towards something instead of just dwelling on what you don't want.

Your mind is like a taxi driver; it will take you wherever you want to go. All you have to do is tell it your destination. If you use an away-from strategy, you are telling the taxi driver where you don't want to go. That will only confuse him because he will not know where to take you.

The same thing happens to your powerful mind if you only tell it what you don't want; it will be confused and take you nowhere.

We can spend years listing all that we don't want, when in fact we are just avoiding admitting what we do want. The time we spend listing things we don't want is time wasted.

Going forward, every time you find yourself saying, "I don't want this" or "I don't want that," stop for a second and think of what you do want instead. That will turn your life around and will get you to where you want to go faster and more efficiently, guaranteed!

All right. You've now identified the six most important things for you in a job. You've also refined that list into powerful statements of what you **do want**.

Now, let's refine this further, and get even closer to knowing your career code. Ready?

PHASE II: DISCOVERING YOUR SELF-LEADERSHIP CODE
Your Six Most Important Job Requirements: Ultra Focus

"Simplicity is the ultimate sophistication."
Leonardo da Vinci

We will now laser focus your job requirements for even easier manifestation into the world. It's easy to create what you want when you have crystalline clarity and an unambiguous ultra focus.

Look at the list you just made of your six most important job requirements. Now take each statement and condense it into one or two words. Look at each statement and ask yourself: What is the simplest form of this statement?

For example, "I want fun projects that excite me" would convert to, "exciting projects." If you wrote "Make lots of money," convert it to "money," "pay," or "compensation."

As before, it may take you a minute to distill these statements, but that is what you are after, the core and essence of what you want.

Write your condensed statements below.

The six things I most want in a job are (in the positive):

1.

2.

3.

4.

5.

6.

Here are some examples of distilled statements of job requirements:

TABLE 1: LIST OF SOME POTENTIAL CAREER CODES

Achievement, advancement, adventure, aesthetics, authority, autonomy, balance, challenge, compensation, competition, creativity, detail work, efficiency, fast pace, flexibility, helping others, independence, influence, integrity, intellectual stimulation, knowledge, leadership, leisure time, location, management, positive atmosphere, power, prestige, public affairs, moral fulfillment, personal growth, good projects, recognition, experience...

Finished? That was pretty challenging, wasn't it? However, I am sure you feel better and more in control now that you have arrived at the core of what's most important to you in a job.

PHASE II: DISCOVERING YOUR SELF-LEADERSHIP CODE
The Power of Simplicity

There is a lot of power in simplicity. Life is complicated enough and the last thing you need is to complicate it even more. Simplicity is elegance, beauty, and efficiency. If you want a happy, productive and unfolding career, aim for simplicity.

One of our flaws as human beings is that we like to take simple things and make them complicated, and to take complicated things and make them even more complicated. The cycle never stops unless we consciously break it.

Your self-leadership code doesn't have to be complicated. In fact, the simpler you make it, the better. The smallest elements on a vault are usually numbers or letters. The smallest elements of your career code are single words.

The goal of this book is to make it easy for you to have a fulfilling career and life. Every exercise you do takes you further from complexity, chaos, and indecision towards simplicity, focus, and power.

Complexity and confusion go hand in hand. The more you feel like writing paragraphs about what you want, the further you are from the truth. Think of the formula $E=MC^2$ every time you are working on your code. Einstein's genius lay in his ability to simplify complex equations, which could fill encyclopedias, into a simple formula that revolutionized physics. Your code will have power if it's simple and to the point.

You have distilled your career code. Now, let's sharpen it further. Let's prioritize your job requirements and sequence your career code. We are almost there.

PHASE II: DISCOVERING YOUR SELF-LEADERSHIP CODE

Sequence Your Career Code: Prioritize Your Six Most Important Job Requirements

"You are as unique as your fingerprint."

As you might already know, DNA for all life on earth is built through the combination of four different codes. The codes that make a lizard are the same as those that make a chimp and that make you. The only difference is the way they are sequenced or the order in which they are strung together.

The sequence of your self-leadership code, or the order of what is most to least important, will make a dramatic difference in the kind of job you seek and your level of satisfaction. So here we will prioritize your list of requirements.

I use this procedure in my coaching sessions with entry-level employees to top-level executives. They all marvel at its simplicity and power.

For this process, you will need a quiet room and a working space (you'll be putting pieces of paper on the table), six pieces of paper or sticky notes big enough to write your self-leadership code, and a pen.

Let's get started.

1. Do the centering exercise in the introduction.

2. If you need to see a demo of this, visit www.SelfLeadershipGuide. com. Complete the exercise by coming back to this page at any time.

3. Write each of your six job requirements on a small piece of paper or a sticky note.

4. Line up the pieces of paper on the table from the most important to the least important to you (as in the figure below). If you have a hard time deciding which is most important, just pick one and put it on the table.

MOST IMPORTANT

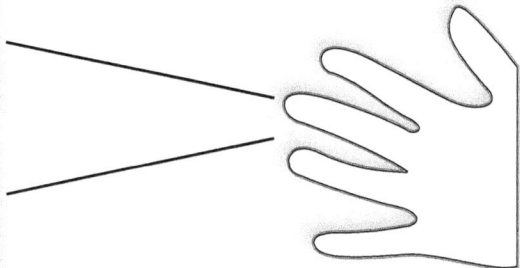

Pay

Respect

Creativity

Career Advancement

Bio Related

Goal Oriented

5. Now place your fingers next to the first code at the bottom of the list.

6. Only look at this code and the one next up in the line.

7. Once you see both, ask yourself this: Which one would I let go of if I had to? This is the most important part; you have to choose one that you are willing to discard. You have to make a conscious decision here and now. Ultimately, you will keep both, but for the purpose of this exercise, you have to make a choice.

8. If your finger is next to the code you would be willing to let go of, move one step forward with your finger. If not, then swap the position of the two codes so that the one you would be willing to give up is now at the bottom of the two.

9. Now your finger should move up one level next to the second code.

10. Only look at this code and the one next up in the line.

MOST IMPORTANT

Pay

Respect

Creativity

Career Advancement

Bio Related

Goal Oriented

LEAST IMPORTANT

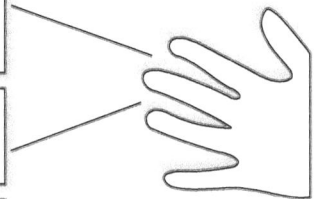

11. Once you see both codes, ask yourself again: **Which one would I let go of if I had to?** (**Note:** Make sure you use exactly the same question as you move through the rest of the exercise.)

12. If your finger is next to the code you would be willing to let go of, move one step forward with your finger. If not, swap the position of the two codes so that the one you would be willing to give up is at the bottom of the two.

13. Now repeat the process until you get to the top of the list.

14. Once you get to the top, repeat the procedure going from top to bottom.

15. Place your finger next to the top code on the list and compare it to the one below it.

16. If your finger is next to the code you would be willing to let go of, swap the position of the two codes so that the one you would be willing to discard is at the bottom of the two. Otherwise, move one code downward towards the bottom of the list.

17. Repeat the process until you get to the bottom of the list.

18. Just note if your code sequence has ended up being different from your initial alignment.

19. Write your code as it appears in the order of most important on the top to least important on the bottom.

My career code in order of priority, from most important to least important, is:

1.

2.

3.

4.

5.

6.

Great! Did you have a hard time choosing one requirement over another? Now that you have your requirements in order, does it make sense why you might not have been happy in a job you had? If your job requirements are met, do you see how much happier you would be?

A study was performed at Duke University in 2000 to ascertain what managers thought was most important to their employees. The results are listed in the table below: "1" being most important. Compare their results to your code. Do you see any similarities? Do you see any differences? Do you see how the differences can cause conflict in the workplace? This demonstrates the importance of knowing your code and its order. If you just rely on management, most likely they will get it wrong.

WHAT YOU WANT FROM YOUR JOB	MANAGER'S RATING
Learning	6
Skills	2
Feeling Good	5
Pay	1
Interesting Work	7
Praise and Appreciation	8
Benefits	4
Security	3

Congratulations! Now you know what is most important to you in a job in order of priority; you know your self-leadership code and its sequence. Now you are ready to open the vault and reap all the career rewards available to you.

By going through this process and identifying what is most important to you in your work environment, you have gone beyond what most professionals would even dream of doing. Now you can plan your career based on what makes you tick. You can pick projects that will fulfill you. You can make work-related decisions with ease and navigate your career with minimal conflict and friction.

Most importantly, your unconscious mind (more about that in a minute) is set to detect what you are interested in and to direct your attention so you can accomplish your career goals with ease and grace.

The Importance of Knowing the Priority of Your Job Requirements or The Sequence of Your Career Code

It takes some work, as you've seen, to know your self-leadership code and its sequence. Yet it is very important, as you'll find in the story about Janet and Mike, my clients who are twins.

Janet and Mike both have *creative projects* and *independence* in their career code. Mike values independence first and creative projects second. Janet is the opposite. She values creative projects first and independence second.

Consequently, Janet chose a career as a winemaker in a local winery. Mike chose marketing consulting. Both are in full pursuit of their respective careers, honoring that which is most important to them in a job first, with other things following.

Both Mike and Janet share two similar codes, yet the order of their values made a huge difference in the jobs they chose. The same applies to you.

Do you sometimes feel conflict around a career decision? Sequencing your code will eliminate any friction you might have.

Mark, another client, valued *job security* and *project variety* at the same level. This got in his way of deciding to leave his secure management job in favor of pursuing a CEO position that offered *project variety.*

One day he wanted variety and another day he wanted security, creating a paralyzing conflict that kept him in indecision. Once he sequenced his code and consciously chose *project variety* over *job security*, he could make a life- and career-changing decision to pursue the CEO position that just opened at his current company. Mark got the position and is now happy working in his dream job based on his code.

When you clearly understand the order of your job requirements, your career code sequence, you will be in a position to make fast and excellent decisions, giving you a distinct career advantage.

Being in the right place at the right time is not enough to succeed anymore; you also need to make the right decisions in the right place at the right time. Once you know your career code, making the right decisions becomes the natural thing to do.

PHASE II: DISCOVERING YOUR SELF-LEADERSHIP CODE
Working Consciously with Your Powerful Unconscious

Your unconscious mind is a powerful tool. If you are not consciously making use of it in your career and job decisions, you are missing out on a superior resource. Knowing clearly what you want in a job, and stating it simply and in order of priority, automatically engages this vast power, the power of your unconscious, locked in the back of your mind.

How Does It Work?

Your mind is divided into two parts, the conscious and the unconscious. A common metaphor used in hypnotherapy is that the mind is like an iceberg; one-third of the iceberg is floating on top of the ocean and two-thirds are floating under. Your conscious mind is the part floating on top and the lower and larger part is your unconscious.

Your unconscious mind's job is to serve you. Knowing your code directs your unconscious to focus on what is important to you and sequencing your code directs it to what to concentrate on first.

Once your unconscious mind knows the code, it will operate behind the scenes and, without you being aware of it, will make things happen for you.

There is a small part of the brain called the reticular activating system (RAS). Once the RAS learns of something important to you, it will scan the environment unconsciously and will bring it to your awareness once it finds it.

Here is a simple example we can all relate to that demonstrates how the unconscious mind works.

Think of the last time you purchased a car. You saw the car you wanted and bought it, and thought to yourself that your car was unique since you hadn't seen it often. Yet once you left the dealership and drove out on the street, you saw many cars just like your new car in exactly the same color. Why didn't you see these cars before? They have always existed and yet you did not notice.

The reason you now see your car everywhere is because once you decided to buy it, the reticular activation system in your brain noted that this car is important to you and will now bring it to your awareness every time it's present in your environment. This is why you will see similar cars to yours everywhere after you buy the car.

Your unconscious mind will act in the same way in support of your career choices. Once you discover and sequence your code, your mind will know what is important to you and the order of importance and will have the RAS work for you in the background. Once it notices something in your environment, it will bring it to your awareness. You will be able not only to see opportunities suited to you that you never saw before, but to act on them with speed and ease to your benefit and satisfaction.

All right. Now that you have identified your six most important job requirements and have them organized in order of priority, you are prepared to improve your situation at your current job or seek a new one.

In this next step, we will move from a general description of your job requirements to specific jobs. We will identify concrete projects, activities, tasks, etc. that match your general job requirements and career code.

When you can identify the specific activities that will make you happy, you can take action to obtain them.

Let's convert your code into concrete, and specific activities.

PHASE III : YOUR SELF-LEADERSHIP CODE IN ACTION:
Match Your Job Requirements, Your Career Code, with Concrete Projects and Activities

Just as your list of job requirements is unique to you, the process and activities required to meet and honor those job requirements are also unique. Each code that you have can be fulfilled in thousands of different ways.

What is important here is to discover your own way to fulfill your code, and the specific activities and concrete projects that will meet your most important career requirements.

For example, if one of your priorities is leadership, this could be expressed in a variety of ways: working as a supervisor, acting as a team leader, managing a project, or a combination of all three.

What will honor your desire for leadership will be very different from another person. This is why it's important to find the exact projects and activities that will fulfill your code.

One time I was called to a conflict management intervention meeting between a winemaker and the production manager of a winery.

The winemaker wanted to have some creative control over the

process and thought that the production manager was not allowing him to do so. In a private meeting with both, I asked the winemaker to express his wishes to the production manager. The winemaker immediately said, "I want some creative control over making the wine." The production manager answered, "I understand and I always allow for that in the process."

Obviously, one of the codes for the winemaker was creative control and the production manager knew that. The disagreement here was on how the code was honored.

It turned out that the winemaker's way of honoring the code was to be allowed to run some taste experiments on the wine from the bottling line. The production manager thought the winemaker was getting his creative control by deciding what batches to be mixed to create the final product.

Once the production manager knew exactly how the winemaker's code could be honored, he was very happy to work something out and the conflict was resolved.

It's vital to know both your code and what activities and projects will honor it. Both are essential to your level of satisfaction and success at what you do.

Telling your manager that you want more leadership roles in the organization is not enough. He or she will find ways to honor your request, but not necessarily as you wish.

Unfortunately, this is very common in organizations and it creates conflict between managers and subordinates all the time. Just like in the winemaker and production manager's story above, requests to honor the code must be followed by requests for specific projects or activities.

Now let's take your list of requirements and identify concrete activities that will fulfill them.

In the space below, on the left side, write your code. Then to the right of your code, list concrete activities, jobs, tasks, projects, etc. that would fulfill it.

YOUR CODE   **ACTIVITIES (GENERAL CRITERIA)**

1.

2.

3.

4.

5.

6.

Here is an example.

YOUR CODE	GENERAL CRITERIA
LEADERSHIP	Leadership role in my group and have direct reports
RESPONSIBILITY	Be responsible for a whole step in a project
INDUSTRY	Biotech Industry
PAY / MONEY	Good Money / Industry Standard
BEING APPRECIATED	I want to feel appreciated in the company I work for
CONTRIBUTION	I want to work on things that have big impact on society and on the organization

Finished? Very good! Now you have a list of specific activities that will make you happy and motivated in a job.

These activities, tasks, projects, etc. that you are after are your goals. You will now take action to create circumstances in which you can do jobs that you love to do.

There are many means, methods, and approaches to achieving goals. Here I will teach you a superior method called The SMART Goals System. This system will make your goals powerful and relevant to your job, career, and future. After all, Abraham Lincoln once said, "A goal properly set is halfway reached." The SMART Goals System will make sure your goals are properly set.

PHASE III : YOUR SELF-LEADERSHIP CODE IN ACTION:
The SMART Goals System:
A Tool for Setting and Achieving Goals

*"The more intensely we feel about an idea or a goal, the more assuredly
the idea, buried deep in our subconscious, will direct us along
the path to its fulfillment."*
Earl Nightingale

You have now identified specific activities arising from your most
important requirements and can take action to pursue them.

In this section, I will share with you a powerful tool for setting
goals, the SMART Goals System. As you already know, setting goals is
necessary if you want to achieve anything in life, so it is important to take
a minute to learn this method.

A good example of the importance of goal setting is the story of
Bruce Lee. Experts agree that Bruce Lee achieved in his thirty-two years
more than a dozen people did in a lifetime. The same experts agree that
his great achievements are based on his powerful goal-setting ability.

> Here is Bruce Lee's personal handwritten goal dated
> January 1969, titled: "My Chief Aim." It reads:
> "I, Bruce Lee, will be the first highest paid
> Oriental....

> ....superstar in the United States. In return I will give the most exciting performances and render the best of quality in the capacity of an actor. Starting in 1970 I will achieve world fame and from then onward till the end of 1980 I will have in my possession $ 10,000,000. I will live the way I please and achieve inner harmony and happiness."
> And he achieved this. How powerful is that!

You might know that goal setting is important, but have no idea what Goals to set. That's normal. Most professionals just set goals for the sake of setting goals. Without knowing your code, setting professional goals is ineffective because it lacks a foundation for motivation.

Your code gives you the purpose behind the goals, so achieving them becomes fulfilling. If you don't set goals based on your code, you are probably setting the wrong goals and I would not be surprised if you give up on them before you achieve them.

We worked on your code first because it will help you connect your goals to your deeper values, which will allow you to experience pleasure working with them. In turn, this will link you to an unstoppable passion that will help you achieve the goals you set.

The goals you are going to set are called SMART code goals, because they will be based on your self-leadership code.

SMART Goals Are Ecological Too

Using Neuro-Linguistic Programming and systemic thinking, we know that a goal that does not take into account its overall consequences (good or bad) is not a very smart goal.

Your goal could affect other areas of your life such as your family, friends, and career, so you must accommodate for this. When you account for the consequences of your goal and know how it's going to impact other areas of your life, your goal is called smart and ecological. So for your goal to be SMART, you need to make sure that it is ecological as well.

Many professionals decide to be a partner in their firm and end up losing their family in the process.

Just like when you build a house on a piece of land and your actions affect its ecology, setting a bad goal could have the same impact on other areas of your life.

Here are the criteria for a goal to be SMART. You will use these criteria to determine if the activities, as goals, you have listed are SMART before you set them firmly.

Smart Goals Criteria

For a goal to be SMART, it has to pass these six conditions:

1. **S**pecific

2. **M**easurable

3. **A**ttainable

4. **R**ealistic

5. **T**imely

6. **E**cological

A SMART Goal Is *Specific*

A specific goal has a much greater chance of being accomplished than a general one.

Consider this. Let's say your goal is to make more money this year. Obviously, that goal is very general and will not work. Your mind will not be able to quantify "more money." Once you set that goal, your unconscious mind, with the help of the RAS system we talked about in the last section, will automatically try to help you to achieve it. Since the goal is general, your unconscious mind will find a general solution.

For example, you are walking down the street and you find a shiny penny. Voilà! You just made more money than you normally do. Your unconscious mind will stop working on the goal because as far as it's concerned, the mission has been accomplished.

Your unconscious mind will help you achieve any goal you tell it to. Be careful what you ask it, because it will find a way to help you get it. To get exactly what you want, make sure you are specific.

To set a specific goal, you must answer the four "W" questions:

Specific Goal Questions
Who: Who is involved?
What: What do I want to accomplish?
Where: In what context?
When: What is my timeframe?

Here's an example. A general goal would be "get a leadership role." A specific goal would be "lead a complete project in my department for a whole year."

A SMART Goal Is *Measurable*

Just as your goal has to be specific, it also has to be measurable. If your goal is not measurable, you will never know whether you are getting closer to achieving it. Sometimes you will not even know if you've achieved it already. Making your goal measurable will give you the chance to track your progress and the pleasure of knowing that you've achieved it when you do.

Once a client called me out of the blue and requested a refund for the work we'd done together in the previous month. With panic in my voice, I said, "Sure," and asked for an explanation. The client said that her goal of working with me was to become more assertive, and she did not feel that she had succeeded.

I looked at her file and at how we had stated the goal and to my surprise, it was the following: "At the end of my working relationship with Peter on May 30 2002, I will be able to call whoever I think wronged me and demand a corrective action." I read her goal to her aloud on the phone. There was silence at the end of the line, then loud laughter. She'd just realized that her goal had been achieved and that she had just done something she could never have done before.

I am glad I helped my client articulate her goal in a specific, measurable way because it allowed her to realize her success.

Without a specific, measurable form, a goal is just a dream and you never know whether or not you've achieved it.

Peter Drucker, the famous business consultant, once said that whatever can be measured can be managed. Do yourself a favor and make sure all your goals are measurable.

To make sure your goal is measurable, establish concrete, "sensory" criteria for evaluating your progress.

Ask yourself: How will I know that I have achieved my goal? What sensory-based evidence will I have? What will I see, hear, and even say?

Procedure for making your goal MEASURABLE:
1. Make sure each goal is stated in sensory-based language.
2. What will you see, hear, and feel when you achieve it?

Here's an example. An immeasurable goal would be "get promoted." A measurable goal would be "get promoted to E1 level."

A SMART Goal Is *Attainable*

You can't set goals and expect somebody else to achieve them for you. The goal must be self-initiated and attainable for it to work. If your goal is for your manager to be nice to you, it is not attainable because you can't set goals for somebody else. A better goal, for example, would be: "Have a conversation with my manager next week and discuss the way he treats me."

In a full-day training I was doing for an organization, a woman announced that her goal was to have one of her coworkers write a transition plan before he retired. Can you see how this goal is set up for failure from the start? Obviously, that woman can't control her coworker's actions. If he doesn't produce the transition plan, she will not accomplish her goal. What would be a better goal here?

Your goals should be self-initiated and self-directed to be attainable. You can never set goals for other people and expect them to work. You can only set goals that you can control.

Procedure to make sure your goal is ATTAINABLE:
1. Ask yourself: "Am I the only person responsible for initiating and completing the goal?"

Here's an example. An unattainable goal would be "have my manager like me." An attainable one would be "learn rapport skills and use them when interacting with my manager."

A SMART Goal Is *Realistic*

Henry Ford once said: "Whether you believe you can or you can't, you are right." You have to believe that you can achieve your goal. If you say your goal is to make a million dollars and you don't believe that you can, you will not be able to get that amount. Your beliefs reside in your subconscious mind, and they are the default setting. In order to achieve your goals, you need to make those goals realistic by setting them within.

To achieve a goal, it must be realistic in terms of your expectations. You and only you know what is realistic for you. It is usually good to stretch a little beyond what you think is realistic so you can actualize more of your potential, but too much of a gap can stop you in your tracks.

For example, if you are starting out as an entry-level employee at General Electric, what is the possibility of you becoming the CEO in three months? If that is not realistic for you, you need to pick a more realistic goal.

A close friend once told me that in his village in India, the locals raised elephants to do work. They would catch a baby elephant and would tie it to a tree with a small rope. When the baby elephant tried to cut the rope, its leg would hurt. Soon the baby elephant learned that it couldn't cut the rope and it would hurt if it tried. The baby elephants grew into massive adult elephants and the only thing holding them to the tree was that small rope they were tied with when they were young. They never tried to break it because they believed that they couldn't.

The same thing happens to us. We sometimes learn to believe things that limit us and we may need to challenge what we think is possible or not possible.

For example, some people don't believe that they can be happy at work and still make a living. Others believe that work does not have to be fulfilling. These are the small ropes that we need to break to free ourselves and be happy in our lives and careers.

Sometimes, some lucky elephants break the small rope by accident. These are the elephants you can't tie back to the same tree again, because they have realized that the rope is easy to break.

Procedure to make sure your goal is REALISTIC
1. Ask yourself: Has somebody else achieved the goal?
2. Is it humanly possible?
3. Do you believe it can happen?
4. If the answer is Yes to any of these questions, your goal is realistic.

A SMART Goal Is _Timely_

A goal should be grounded within a timeframe. With no timeframe tied to the goal, there will be no sense of urgency. If you want to get a raise, when do you want it? "Someday" won't work. However, if you anchor it within a timeframe, "by April 1, 2040," let's say, you've set your unconscious mind in motion to begin working on the goal. If you don't set a deadline, your unconscious mind will interpret this as unimportant and will put it aside to work on other things.

To make sure your code goals are achievable, they must fit in a time-frame, or they are just dreams floating in your mind. The moment you put a deadline on a goal is the moment you make it real and important.

Ensure all your code goals have a time stamp on them.

Procedure to make sure your goal is TIMELY:
1. Ask yourself: Does the goal have a specific time of completion?
2. If yes, then it is timely.

Here's an example. An untimely goal would be "lead a complete project in my department for a whole year." A timely goal would be "lead a complete project in my department for a whole year, starting January 2040."

A SMART Goal Is *Ecological*

Finally, you have to check if your goal is ecological. To be ecological, the goal must satisfy two criteria.

1. The goal must be stated in the positive because the subconscious mind doesn't know how to interpret negatives.
2. The goal must be aligned with your other goals and your life.

Positive Check

When you say your goal is "NOT to get hurt," your subconscious mind has to imagine being hurt, so it's better to say your goal is "to be safe." Also, remember when we talked about a "towards" strategy as opposed to an "away-from" strategy? You want to use a "towards" strategy in your life, so goals should reflect this by being stated in the positive.

A positive goal will keep you going forward with focus, clarity, and speed. A goal set in the negative will lead to more chaos, frustration, and ambiguity. Choose the towards approach and always convert your goals into the positive.

Here is an example. A negative goal is, "I don't want to be an engineer forever." A positive statement is, "I want to become a firm supervisor."

Alignment Check

The second criterion for goal ecology is that the goal must be aligned with your other goals.

For example, if one of your goals is to be a supervisor at a CPA firm by 2040, you can't have another goal of being a full-time Olympic swimmer by the same date. These two goals could be in conflict unless you find a creative way to reconcile them.

Conflict between goals is not limited to the career ones you just set; you also need to check for possible conflict with your other life goals as well.

For example, if you want to become a partner at a CPA firm, you know that you might be expected to put in many hours and that this might affect your social or family goals.

To make sure that your goals align, you need to either be strict with what goals you set, or be creative with how you resolve the conflict between them.

If you must choose between two conflicting goals, then do it. If you can work out a creative alternative, then do that. However, never leave two conflicting goals to drift and expect to achieve either one of them.

The conflict will drain your energy. It will unfocus your efforts and you will find that you will not be happy even if you achieve your goals.

The key to successful, ecological goals is to have them work in alignment and not in conflict.

ECOLOGY Questionnaire:

Is the goal stated in the positive?

Is the goal right for you at this point in your life?

Is there anything you might lose by achieving this goal?

- Relationships?
- Money?
- Time?
- Family?
- Something else?
- How are you going to account for any losses?
- Is there something that might get in your way of achieving your goal?
- What is your plan for overcoming obstacles?

So here you are with a new powerful tool. Now, let's put this tool to work on achieving your career goals.

PHASE III : YOUR SELF-LEADERSHIP CODE IN ACTION:
Taking Action to Job Satisfaction!

Now that you are armed with a tool to set and achieve your goals, we will create a list of goals that are smart, actionable, and achievable.

By achieving your goals, you will get what you want, satisfaction in your career, and happiness and peace of mind in your life.

For your convenience, below is a succinct list of SMART goals criteria. Or you can download a printable list at www.SelfLeadershipGuide.com.

SMART Goals Criteria

   1. Specific

   2. Measurable

   3. Attainable

   4. Realistic

   5. Timely

   6. Ecological

Specific Goal Questions

Who: Who is involved?

What: What do I want to accomplish?

Where: What is my context?

When: What is my time frame?

Procedure for making your goal MEASURABLE:

Make sure each goal is stated in sensory-based language.

What will you see, hear, and feel when you achieve it?

Procedure to make sure your goal is ATTAINABLE:

Ask yourself: Am I the only person responsible for initiating and completing the goal?

Procedure to make sure your goal is REALISTIC:

Ask yourself: Has somebody else achieved the goal?

Is it humanly possible?

Do you believe it can happen?

If the answer is Yes to any of these questions, your goal is realistic.

Procedure to make sure your goal is TIMELY:

Ask yourself: Does the goal have a specific time of completion?

If yes, then it is timely.

ECOLOGY Questionnaire:

Is the goal stated in the positive?

Is the goal right for you at this point in your life?

Is there anything that you might lose by achieving this goal?

- Relationships?
- Money?
- Time?
- Family?
- Something else?
- How are you going to account for any losses?

- Is there something that might get in your way of achieving your goal?
- What is your plan for overcoming obstacles?

All right. We are now ready to get started and turn your goals into SMART goals.

In the space provided below, once again write your list of job requirements in order of priority under the heading Career Code.

Then, under the Activities column, write what you had written down before as the activities that would express your job requirements.

Now, in the column called SMART Code Goal, take each of your Activities and translate it into SMART Goals by ask yourself the SMART Goals questions: Is this goal specific, measurable, attainable, realistic, timely and ecological?

CAREER CODE   ACTIVITIES (GENERAL CRITERIA)   SMART CODE GOAL

1.

2.

3.

4.

5.

6.

Here's an example of job requirements, turned into activities, turned into SMART goals.

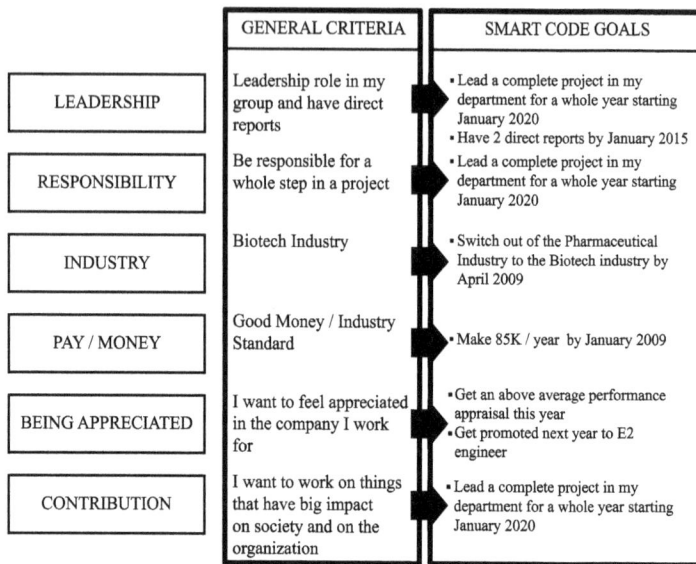

	GENERAL CRITERIA	SMART CODE GOALS
LEADERSHIP	Leadership role in my group and have direct reports	• Lead a complete project in my department for a whole year starting January 2020 • Have 2 direct reports by January 2015
RESPONSIBILITY	Be responsible for a whole step in a project	• Lead a complete project in my department for a whole year starting January 2020
INDUSTRY	Biotech Industry	• Switch out of the Pharmaceutical Industry to the Biotech industry by April 2009
PAY / MONEY	Good Money / Industry Standard	• Make 85K / year by January 2009
BEING APPRECIATED	I want to feel appreciated in the company I work for	• Get an above average performance appraisal this year • Get promoted next year to E2 engineer
CONTRIBUTION	I want to work on things that have big impact on society and on the organization	• Lead a complete project in my department for a whole year starting January 2020

How did that go? Was it easier or harder than you thought? Do you feel satisfied with the SMART goals you have created?

You now have a set of professional goals based on a solid foundation: SMART goals that honor your career code. The foundation is your code. It will give you purpose, inspire you, and motivate you to accomplish your goals.

I recommend that you photocopy your career code planner above and keep it in your wallet or purse as a reminder of what you want. This will reinforce your unconscious mind and set you up for magic to happen. Jim Cary once revealed on *The Oprah Show* that before he was famous, he wrote a ten million dollar check to himself dated November 1995 and carried it with him all the time. Jim pulled out the deteriorating check occasionally as a reminder of what he wanted. In October 1995, two years after he wrote the check, Jim Cary got a role in the movie *Dumb and Dumber* with a total compensation of ten million dollars.

This is the magic of writing down your goals and reviewing them regularly.

By the way, if you examine Jim Cary's check you will notice that it fits the whole SMART Goals criteria; it's specific, measurable, attainable, realistic and timely.

PHASE III : YOUR SELF-LEADERSHIP CODE IN ACTION:
Your Current Job and Your Code: Does Your Current Job Honor Your Career Code? Are Your Most Important Job Requirements Being Met in Your Current Job?

In the last section, you created SMART code goals that will get you what you want in a job. In this section, you will take a look at your current job and will see to what extent it fulfills your most important job requirements.

To get the most out of your current job, you need to know which of your job requirements are being honored and which are not. Once you know what job requirements are not being honored, you can take action to honor them and maximize your happiness and satisfaction.

If you are happy at your job, chances are your code is being honored every single day. If you are not happy, your code is not being honored.

Let's get started.

In the left column of the table below, list your job requirements. In the right column, rate whether each requirement is being honored at your current job. Use a scale of 1–10, 10 meaning that your job requirement is honored 100%.

When you're done, take the additional step of giving a 1–10 rating of your overall satisfaction in your job.

MY JOB REQUIREMENTS MY CAREER CODE	MY SATISFACTION LEVEL ON A SCALE OF 1-10
1.	
2.	
3.	
4.	
5.	
6.	
7. Overall satisfaction rating on a scale of 1-10	

For example, if leadership is one of your requirements and you are not getting to express it in your current position, you would give it a 1. If it were being honored once in a while, you would give it a 2 or a 3, and if it were honored all the time, you would give it a 10.

Here is what an evaluation might look like. It's an actual evaluation from one of my clients.

MY JOB REQUIREMENTS MY CAREER CODE	MY SATISFACTION LEVEL ON A SCALE OF 1-10
1. Leadership	8
2. Responsibility	7
3. Industry	3
4. Pay / Money	5
5. Being Appreciated	6
6. Contribution	2
7. Overall satisfaction rating on a scale of 1-10	5

In this example, you can see that the overall satisfaction level in the job is a 5. You can tell that the codes of "contribution" and "industry" are not being honored much. Because this data is coming from one of my clients, I know that by working on honoring these two codes more often, her satisfaction level jumped to 8.

Now let's look at the evaluation of your current job. What did you discover? Are your job requirements being honored to a good degree, or not? Your overall satisfaction will depend on how many of your codes are being honored. Do you see the correlation between the two?

Your ultimate goal is to honor all your codes and bring all of them to 10. This will affect your attitude, your motivation, and your productivity. Additionally, the quality of your work will improve tremendously.

Reflection Questions

1. Do you see the relationship between your job code and satisfaction?

2. How many of your codes are honored to the fullest?

3. Is it possible to have a code that will never be honored at your current position?

4. How does this change your perspective on your job?

5. What are the codes of your coworkers and how many of them are being honored?

6. Is your boss's code being honored?

7. Share your insights on this book's website, www.SelfLeadershipGuide.com and get extra resources.

Is It Possible to Have 10 for All Your Job Requirements and Still Not be Satisfied?

The answer is Yes. This means that you didn't make an accurate assessment of your important job requirements.

Sometimes we choose a requirement based on what is expected of us. Some people might pick leadership because they think that they are supposed to pick it as one of their job codes and not because they truly desire it. If that's you, then go back and redo the exercises. Sometimes we have to peel through some layers to get to what is really important. Doing the exercises the second time around will be easier.

Life's too short to live based on other people's requirements. You must decipher your own code and go after what you want and what makes you happy and successful. Living based on somebody else's code will not satisfy you in the end. Enjoy a career founded on your own unique values and reap all the rewards available to you.

A client of mine just retired from a forty-year career as an unhappy CPA and is now starting a happy new career as a music teacher. He told me after our first session that he wished he had known about his code forty years ago because it could have saved him so much stress, anxiety, and frustration. Of course, as the saying goes, it's never too late and it's better now than never.

Satisfaction Level and Performance

Numerous studies show the correlation between success and performance to the level of satisfaction at work. One such recent study was performed by Thomas Wright, a psychology researcher at Kansas State University. The results showed that when employees have high levels of job satisfaction, they perform better and are less likely to leave their job. Of course, you know this intuitively. You know that you would work harder and perform better in a job that you liked than in one you didn't like.

Fortunately, your job satisfaction is linked to your code. Fulfill your code and you will be happy, productive, and successful at your current and future jobs.

There are many ways to approach honoring your code. In the section below, we will explore three strategies that may be appropriate for you and your situation.

PHASE III : YOUR SELF-LEADERSHIP CODE IN ACTION:
Three Strategies to Achieve Fulfillment and Empowerment at Work: What to do when Your Most Important Job Requirements Are Not Being Fulfilled in Your Current Job

*"**Strategy** without tactics is the slowest route to victory. Tactics without **strategy** is the noise before defeat."*
Sun Tzu

You may just have discovered that your current job does not meet your requirements. What do you do? How do you go about getting your job requirements met?

In this section, I will show you strategies to start changing your current job situation.

Now, take a moment to go back to the exercise where you identified your SMART goals.

It is in pursuing and meeting these goals in your current job that you will meet your most important job requirements, fulfill your career code, and obtain job satisfaction.

Here's a space for you to write them again for easy reference.

JOB REQUIREMENTS	PROJECTS, ACTIVITIES, TASKS	SMART GOALS
1.		
2.		
3.		
4.		
5.		
6.		

The most important question is: Which SMART code goal should you start with in order to raise your potential for motivation, satisfaction, and success at work?

There are many approaches to this question and we will explore them here.

The Squeaky-Wheel Strategy

The squeaky wheel gets the grease. You've heard that before and it implies that the wheel that makes the most noise gets the attention.

Looking at your evaluation, which job requirement is least honored? Which one is causing the most dissatisfaction? This is the one to work on first.

This strategy works well when you have a small number of dishonored codes. You tackle the codes by fulfilling the goals and you are done. If you have a short list of unmet requirements, you can get started by implementing your goals for each particular code.

However, if you have a variety of unmet job requirements, you can use another strategy, The leveraged strategy.

The Leveraged Strategy

To demonstrate the Leveraged Strategy, let's look again at my client's job assessment.

MY JOB REQUIREMENTS MY CAREER CODE	MY SATISFACTION LEVEL ON A SCALE OF 1-10
1. Leadership	8
2. Responsibility	7
3. Industry	3
4. Pay / Money	5
5. Being Appreciated	6
6. Contribution	2
7. Over all Satisfaction rating on a scale of 1-10	5

Notice that "contribution" is the least honored Code for my client. If she were to follow the squeaky wheel strategy, she would tackle this code first. Looking at her SMART code goals, you can see that the goal that needs to be honored is:

"Lead a complete project in my department for a whole year starting January 2009"

GENERAL CRITERIA	SMART CODE GOALS
LEADERSHIP — Leadership role in my group and have direct reports	• Lead a complete project in any department for a whole year starting January 2020 • Have 2 direct reports by January 2015
RESPONSIBILITY — Be responsible for a whole step in a project	• Lead a complete project in my department for a whole year starting January 2020
INDUSTRY — Biotech Industry	• Switch out of the Pharmaceutical Industry to the Biotech industry by April 2009
PAY / MONEY — Good Money / Industry Standard	• Make 85K / year by January 2009
BEING APPRECIATED — I want to feel appreciated in the company I work for	• Get an above average performance appraisal this year • Get promoted next year to E2 engineer
CONTRIBUTION — I want to work on things that have big impact on society and on the organization	• Lead a complete project in my department for a whole year starting January 2020

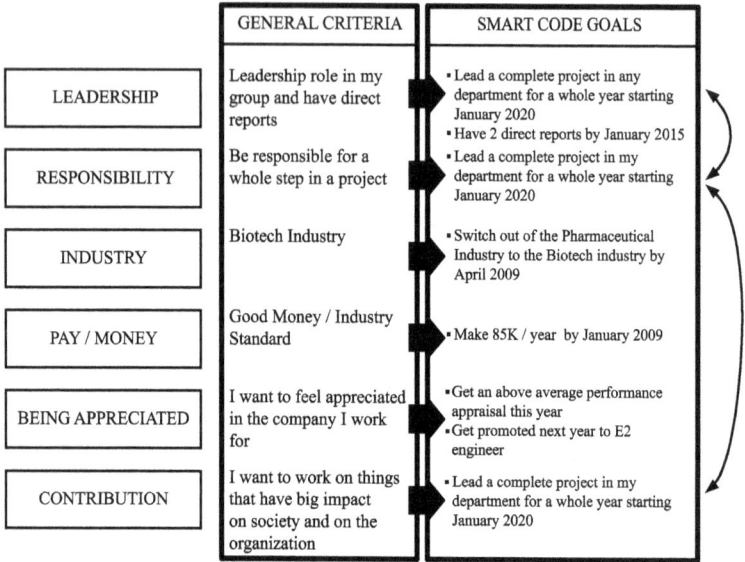

The leveraging strategy is like hitting two birds with one stone. You tackle the one goal that will honor multiple codes at the same time.

From the example above, you can see that the goal of "leading a project in my department for a whole year starting January 2009" honors three codes at once. Pursuing and achieving that one goal will help honor her code faster and maximize her job satisfaction.

This is by far my favorite strategy to use with myself and with my clients. You just have to get creative when you pick the goals to start with, so that you can build leverage into your system of achievement.

If you can't find ways to come up with leveraged goals, then no worries, you can still utilize the other strategies to derive satisfaction from working towards achieving your code goals.

The Pink Elephant Strategy

What if you have a requirement that can't be honored in your current job or even in the industry? You are simply in the wrong industry. If that's your situation, you might have a pink elephant code that drains any fulfillment and joy out of your career.

I had a client with a pink elephant in her code. She was employed in the pharmaceutical industry, but what she really wanted to do was work in the biotech industry. The code obviously couldn't be honored in her current position.

When you have a pink elephant in your code, you might want to pretend that it doesn't exist and ignore it for a while. But ultimately, this pink elephant has to be addressed; it's taking up huge space in your psyche.

The first thing you need to do when you have a pink elephant in your code is to admit it, at least to yourself. If you are working as an engineer and one of your requirements can only be honored as a graphic designer, you have a pink elephant and you might as well admit it. Only when you do this can you begin to deal with it.

Once you admit that you have a pink elephant, you might want to decide whether to deal with it first or to put it aside until you try to honor the other requirements.

I say put it aside because sometimes when people start honoring the rest of their code in their current position, they tend to discover that their industry or job is not so bad after all. Fulfilling the other items on their list tends to elevate their satisfaction and they tend to stick around longer. Sometimes, they even change their mind about their current position and industry.

Yoke wanted to get out of her sales job into manufacturing. But after working on her other codes, she discovered that she loved her job after all. Though her goal of working in manufacturing initially prompted her to run away, once she found her source of happiness at work by honoring the other codes, she decided to stay in her sales job.

However, if for any reason you want to change your industry first, then that's your choice. Just make sure you do your homework. Find out about the industry and the company. Find out about the managers with whom you will be working. Make sure you ask specific questions in your interviews to determine if the company to which you are applying has the potential to fulfill your career codes. If they can't help you honor your code, you will be wasting your time. If they can help you, you will do fine. I just don't want you to change your job and industry to find yourself in a worse situation than when you started.

Now take a look at your list of met and unmet job requirements.

1. Do you have a squeaky wheel on your list? Will you work to satisfy this job requirement first?

2. Is there one job requirement that you can fulfill that will immediately satisfy a few others? Can you effectively apply a leveraged strategy?

3. Do you have a pink elephant? What will you do? Will you attempt to meet your other job requirements and see if you are happier in your position? Or will you seek a position in a new industry?

Now that you have a good assessment of what you need to do, in the next section, I will show you some communication skills you can use to successfully negotiate and obtain your goals.

PHASE III : YOUR SELF-LEADERSHIP CODE IN ACTION:
Talking Your Way to Success and Satisfaction:
Sharpen Your Communication Skills

*"Skill in the art of **communication** is crucial to a leader's success. He can accomplish nothing unless he can communicate effectively."*
Norman Allen

Knowing how to communicate successfully will help you achieve your goals. How you say things to people will either elicit their support and cooperation or put them on the defensive.

Good communication skills are imperative for success. You can learn them and use them to achieve your goals, and can apply them to create much more fulfilling and harmonious relationships in your life.

At this point you know what will make you fulfilled in a job. You might be considering changing industries, switching jobs, or tweaking the job you currently have.

In this chapter, I will give you tools that will help you go to your manager and talk to him or her successfully about the changes you would like to see happen in your work.

Managers Don't Know What Makes You Happy in a Job Unless You Tell Them

Remember the Duke University study of managers I mentioned earlier? Here I will elaborate on that study.

In the study, managers chose pay as the employees' number one job requirement. Skills improvement was requirement number two.

The study went on to survey the employees. It turned out that pay and improving skills were not even close to the top two most important job requirements.

Managers operate on the assumption that employees want higher pay and better skills as a default because they have no idea what their employees actually want. Your current manager is probably the same way.

If you are unhappy at work and don't feel productive, most likely your manager feels the same way about you. Managers are human beings and they can detect your dissatisfaction. As managers, they feel obligated to do something about it. First, they try to bribe you with a bonus or a reward, but that does not work, so they try to punish you by giving you smaller raises or bonuses and of course, that does not work either. Finally, they just give up and expect the bare minimum. As long as you clock in on time, clock out on time, and do your tasks, you are okay.

You know that pay alone does not fulfill you in the long term and so do the managers, but they don't know any other way to raise your satisfaction and productivity. When managers don't know what to do, they resort to the default setting.

Your best bet for satisfaction at work is to change the default setting.

Your manager does not know your code. I am even going to bet that he or she does not even know his or her own code. So don't expect that your manager will pick the right projects for you, or help you manage your time at work better, or even give you the right career advice.

Everything your manager does is nothing but guesswork, unless you inform him or her about what makes you tick, what motivates you, what you want, what your code is, and what goals you need to fulfill.

In light of this, it would be very wise to let your manager in on what you've been up to lately. Give him or her some clues to what you want and how he or she can help you reach your full potential.

Now is the time to begin taking responsibility for your career and start managing your manager.

The default setting can be changed by simply having a conversation with your manager. Thoughts like, "It's too late now," or "He should know this already" do not help your case and only reinforce the default setting.

It's time to be hopeful, it's time to be optimistic, and it's time to change that old default setting for good. It starts with an honest conversation with your manager. Just follow one of the two formulas below and your life and career will change for the better.

Direct Assertive Formula

As the name implies, this formula gets to the heart of the matter right away. You tell your manager the situation, take responsibility for your actions, and then inform your manager exactly how to motivate and inspire you by honoring your job requirements.

Here is the formula with examples.

1. State the situation without blame or judgment.

I want to talk with you because I have not been feeling motivated at work lately (motivated can be replaced with words like happy, productive, successful, satisfied, etc.).

2. Acknowledge that the manager tried his/her best and take responsibility for your own motivation.

I know that you are doing your best to keep me motivated and it has not been working and I just realized that it's my fault. I have not taken the time to let you know what makes me motivated.

3. Tell the manager exactly what needs to happen and leave room for his/her contribution.

In order to be motivated, I need your help on getting promoted to an Engineer 2 position. I realize that I need to do some work to get there and I need your help and guidance to make the process faster.

4. Be open to the manager's input and make adjustments to your goals.

I say be open because sometimes out of the discussion with your manager come great ideas that are even better than the ones you've created already.

Here's your opportunity to practice talking to your manager. Choose one important issue you would like to address with your manager and write what you will say to him or her.

1. State your situation without blame or judgment.

2. Acknowledge that the manager tried his/her best and take responsibility for your motivation. Say it in your own words.

3. Tell the manager exactly what needs to happen and leave room for his/her contribution.

4. Are you willing to be open to your manager's input? Expect the best from the situation.

Did you successfully identify what you wanted to say and express it without blame or judgment? Do you feel comfortable receiving your manager's input? Have you opened your mind to the possibility that you might have even better opportunities than you envisioned?

All right, let's go to the next tool. You can see if this approach is more appropriate for your current needs.

Indirect Assertive Formula

Using this formula, you would start by explaining the process and after that you would ask for your needs to be met. You would state that you are investigating how to make yourself more motivated and productive at work so you can contribute more to the company. Then you would share your insight with the manager, followed by a direct request. Here is the formula with examples.

1. Explain the process.

I've been reading a book about self-leadership at work and found a couple of ways I can increase my productivity, motivation, and contribution here. I wanted to share them with you to get your input.

2. Share your findings.

I've found that I need to be working on some specific goals to keep me moving forward, motivated, and productive. One of them is to work on becoming an Engineer 2 by next year.

3. Ask for the manager's input and support.

I need your help to make this goal a reality.

4. Be open to the manager's guidance.

If this approach expresses more accurately how you've been feeling and what you need in a job, try writing below, in your own words, this conversation.

1. Explain the process.

2. Share your findings.

3. Ask for and be open to the manager's input and support.

If you want things to change at work, you need to change your manager's default setting. The only civil way to do this is to have a conversation with him or her. Choose the approach that will best express your needs at this time.

Once you start to communicate this way with your managers, they will love you for it. Managers are used to hearing complaints and getting blame for all the horrible things employees are suffering. It will be a breath of fresh air for them to hear that you take responsibility for your own career and propose solutions to your challenges.

By knowing what you want and sharing your requests with your managers, you will be farther ahead in your career than most people. Knowing your job requirements, your code, is the first step; actively seeking to honor your code by setting goals, pursuing them, and having conversations around them is the second. The third step is to lead others by the code.

PHASE III : YOUR SELF-LEADERSHIP CODE IN ACTION:
The Next Step:
Be the Ultimate Leader: Lead by the Code!

"The essence of leadership is self-leadership."
Peter Khoury

When you know your career code and recognize that every person has his or her own, you cross the threshold to becoming the ultimate leader.

By helping others discover and fullfill their code, you become the leader with whom everyone wants to work. You will have dedicated and loyal employees who will work with you because they want to, not because they have to. You will have people working with you who are productive, happy, and purposeful, and that in turn will make you productive, happy, and purposeful. Leading teams will be fun and fulfilling.

Your first step to leading by the code is to figure out your own code and put it into action. In airplanes they tell you to put on your oxygen mask first before you attempt to help others. The same thing applies here. You have to figure out your code and start honoring it before you try to help others honor theirs. By figuring out your code and acting on it, you gain the skill and motivation to help others.

Once you know your code and you've put it into action, you can start working with your employees to help them fulfill their career code.

You can start by making a photocopy of the code sheet and filling it out with each employee. Give him/her a copy and keep a copy for yourself. Your one-on-one sessions will be based on the code sheet.

Once you start working with employees based on their code, there will be no room for guessing. Every project you delegate to them will help them achieve something on their code goal sheet. You will have a window inside your employees' head. You will know exactly what they want and you will do your best to help them achieve it. Suddenly people will not view their work as a chore, a way just to make an income, but as a means to achieving happiness, fulfillment, and success.

Below is a step-by-step action plan for you to start leading by the code. Apply the procedure with each employee and refer to it in each one-on-one session you conduct.

Leading by the Code Action Plan

1. Prepare a code action sheet for each employee you have (see additional blank copies in the appendix).

JOB REQUIREMENTS FOR (EMPLOYEE NAME	PROJECTS, ACTIVITIES, TASKS	SMART GOALS
1.		
2.		
3.		
4.		
5.		
6.		

2. Explore with each employee, individually, his/her job criteria by asking the following question: What is important to you in your job?

   Note: This is similar to the process you've gone through.

3. Narrow down the list to the six most important requirements in a job by asking the employee to go through the list. Make sure he/she picks the most important requirements.

4. Convert the "don't want" statements into "do want" statements (and explain the reasons why). Make sure you understand that section well.

5. Once you have a list of "want" statements, make sure you condense them into simple one- or two-word requirements.

6. Now ask your employee to organize them from the most to the least important and go through the prioritization process from section 6.

7. Once you have the code in sequence, write it down on the code action sheet and congratulate your employee for getting this far.

8. Now brainstorm activities, projects, tasks, etc. that will honor his/her code. It's your job as a leader to help the employee come up with activities that will align with the company and department vision.

9. Document the activities in the job code action planner.

10. From the activities list, generate SMART goals to track progress and measure results. Make sure the SMART goals support company and department goals.

11. Document the SMART goals in the job code action planner.

12. Make a copy for the employee and keep a copy on file.

13. Go over the employee's goals during each one-on-one session with you and make sure he/she is on track.

Congratulations! Now you have helped each of your employees create goals and activities that both support the company and department's mission and that are personally relevant and motivating. You don't have to guess what employees want anymore to make them happy and productive at work. All you have to do is just ask them and go through the simple process provided. Then you can assign them activities that will enrich their careers and yours.

Managers that apply this strategy say that it's the best thing they've done since they've read *The One Minute Manager*. This is a simple and effective approach to managing for results.

Conclusion: You Are not a Lobster

> *"A lobster when left high and dry among the rocks, has not instinct and energy enough to work his way back to the sea, but waits for the sea to come to him. If it does not come, he remains where he is and dies, although the slightest effort would enable him to reach the waves, which are perhaps within a yard of him.* **The world is full of human lobsters: Men stranded on the rocks of indecision and procrastination, who, instead of putting forth their own energies, are waiting for some grand billow of good fortune to set them afloat.**"
>
> Dr. Orrison Swett Marden
>
> **If you got this far, you are not a lobster...**

Dan Kennedy, one of the most successful direct marketers in the world, once said that if he had to boil down his career success secret to something, it would be this: control = responsibility.

Everyone wants control over his or her career and future, yet it's hard to find those who want to take responsibility for all aspects of their lives. By discovering your self-leadership code, you have assumed responsibility and thus control over your career. You have gone beyond 99.9% of all professionals. You are no longer dependent on your manager to find what makes you happy and motivated. You know exactly what makes you tick and you know how to get it. Congratulations!

Armed with this knowledge and control, you can put your code into action within your current job or in a new one. Either way, you have all the tools you need to get whatever makes you happy and excited in your work.

One key quality cannot be overemphasized: Action.

When it comes to controling your career, taking action is the key. You can take the knowledge you've received from this book and be content that you've gained a lot of insight.

Alternatively, you can use this knowledge to take action and get what you want. It's your choice! I recommend the action route because this is what brings the ultimate results.

Take action to escape from prison or else you will remain there. I am not talking about a real prison here; I am talking about the imaginary prison we build for ourselves in our brains.

We set limits on what we can and can't do. We convince ourselves that things will never change, and we settle in a boring job when in fact, escape is a conversation, a phone call, or a résumé submission away.

My first job in the biotech industry was at a small lab. It violated every single self-leadership code I cherished. I tried to communicate with my manager and things improved tremendously but the violations were major and beyond repair. One day on my break, I found a job posted online in which I was interested. I did my research and made a phone call from the lab to the hiring manager. I got an interview the same day and later got the job, all because I decided to escape from the prison of my mind and take action.

I had to put aside my false beliefs that managers don't like it when you call, or that it's hard to move to another job in this industry.

What is your next action step? Do you need to schedule an appointment with your boss? Do you need to build your résumé? Do you need to start managing and leading by the code? Now it's your move.

In this book, you were also given tools to use the self-leadership code with your direct reports. True leadership starts with self-leadership. By knowing your career code and by applying it consistently, you set yourself on the path of true leadership. By knowing what motivates you and what motivates others, you can become a natural leader in anything you do.

If you think about the people who have influenced you in the past, you will find that they used your code. Being able to influence people and have them be happy and motivated to change is the ultimate sign of leadership.

It's easy to have interesting work as long as you know what you want. Your self-leadership code always pinpoints this. It's possible that your self-leadership code might change over time, yet by knowing the process outlined in this book, you will always be able to discover it again and put it into action.

Make sure you keep this book with you throughout your journey and stay true to yourself.

Resource Guide

The following is a list of resources that will enhance your ability to get what you want, as well as your awareness and application of the self-leadership principles I have outlined.

General Success Principles

The Power of Focus: How to Hit Your Business, Personal and Financial Targets with Absolute Certainty by Jack Canfield, Mark Victor Hansen and Les Hewitt. Deerfield Beach, FL: Health Communications, Inc., 2000.

The Art of Possibility: Transforming Personal and Professional Life by Rosamund Stone Zander and Benjamin Zander. New York: Penguin, 2000.

Linchpin: Are You Indispensable? by Seth Godin. New York: Portfolio Hardcover. 2010.

The DNA of Success: Know What You Want...To Get What You Want by Jack M. Zufelt. New York: Regan Books, 2002.

The Science of Success: How to Attract Prosperity and Create Life Balance Through Proven Principles by James A. Ray. La Jolla, CA: SunArk Press, 1999.

Success Through a Positive Mental Attitude by Napoleon Hill and W. Clement Stone. Englewood Cliffs, NJ: Prentice-Hall, Inc., 1977.

Think and Grow Rich by Napoleon Hill. New York: Fawcett Crest, 1960.

Napoleon Hill's Keys to Success: The 17 Principles of Personal Achievement edited by Matthew Sartwell. New York: Plume, 1997.

What Makes the Great Great: Strategies for Extraordinary Achievement by Dennis P. Kimbrow, Ph.D. New York: Doubleday, 1997.

The 7 Habits of Highly Effective People by Stephen R. Covey. New York: Fireside/Simon & Schuster, 1989.

The 100 Absolutely Unbreakable Laws of Business Success
by Brian Tracy. San Francisco: Berret-Koehler, 2000.

**Master Success: Create A Life of Purpose, Passion, Peace
and Prosperity** by Bill Fitzpatrick. Natick, MA: American Success
Institute, 2000.

**The Traits of Champions: The Secrets of Championship
Performance in Business, Life and Golf** by Andrew Wood and
Brian Tracy. Provo, UT; Executive Excellence Publishing, 2000.

**The Great Crossover: Personal Confidence in the Age of the
Microchip** by Dan Sullivan, Babs Smith and Michel Negry.
Chicago and Toronto: The Strategic Coach, 1994.

The Seven Spiritual Laws of Success by Deepak Chopra. San
Rafael: Amber-Allen, 1994.

Extreme Success by Richard Fettke. New York: Fireside, 2002.

The Power of Positive Habits by Dan Robey. Miami: Abritt
Publishing Group, 2003.

Unlimited Power by Anthony Robbins. New York: Simon &
Schuster, 1986.

Peak Performers: The New Heroes of American Business by
Charles Garfield. New York: William Morrow and Company, 1986.

Financial Success

The Dynamic Laws of Prosperity by Catherine Ponder. New
York: DeVorss, 2003.

The One Minute Millionaire by Mark Victor Hansen and Robert
G. Allen. New York: Harmony Books, 2002.

The Millionaire Next Door by Thomas J. Stanley and William D.
Danko. New York: Pocket Books, 1996.

**The Courage To Be Rich: Creating A Life of Material and
Spiritual Abundance** by Suze Orman. New York: Riverhead
Books, 1999.

Rich Dad, Poor Dad by Robert Kiyosaki with Sharon L. Lecter.
Paradise Valley, AZ: Tech Press, Inc., 1997.

The Wealthy Barber by David Chilton. Rocklin, CA: Prima Publishing, 1991.

Time Management and Getting Things Done

First Things First by Stephen Covey, A. Roger Merrill and Rebecca R. Merrill. New York: Simon & Schuster, 1996.

Getting Things Done: The ABCs of Time Management by Edwin C. Bliss. New York: Charles Scribner's Sons, 1991.

Doing It Now by Edwin C. Bliss. New York: Macmillan Publishing Company, 1983.

The 10 Natural Laws of Successful Time and Life Management: Proven Strategies for Increased Productivity and Inner Peace by Hyrum W. Smith. New York: Warner Books, 1994.

The Procrastinator's Handbook: Mastering the Art of Doing It Now by Rita Emmett. New York: Walker Publishing Co., 2000.

Getting Things Done: The Art of Stress-Free Productivity by David Allen. New York: Viking, 2001.

The Power of Full Engagement: Managing Energy, Not Time, Is the Key to High Performance and Personal Renewal by Jim Loehr and Tony Schwartz. New York: Free Press, 2004.

Entrepreneurial and Management Success

Drive: The Surprising Truth About What Motivates Us. Daniel H. Pink. New York: Riverhead Hardcover, 2009

The E-Myth Revisited by Michael Gerber. New York: Harper Business, 1995.

1001 Ways to Reward Employees by Bob Nelson. New York: Workman Publishing, 1994.

The One Minute Manager by Kenneth Blanchard and Spencer Johnson. New York: Berkley Books, 1983.

Good to Great: Why Some Companies Make the Leap... and Others Don't, by Jim Collins. New York: Harper Business, 2001.

Inspiration and Motivation

Dare to Win by Jack Canfield and Mark Victor Hansen. New York: Berkley, 1994.

Chicken Soup for the Soul by Jack Canfield and Mark Victor
Hansen. Deefield Beach, FL: Health Communications, Inc., 1993.
It's Not Over Until You Win by Les Brown. New York: Simon &
Schuster, 1997.

About Peter Khoury

Peter Khoury, MBA, CPC, is a speaker, corporate trainer, and certified professional coach. He is also an acclaimed career strategist, and leadership expert.

Peter provides training for organizations such as the California CPA Foundation (CalCPA), the Institute of Supply Management (ISM), the National Association of Purchasing Managers (NAPM), the Charted Property and Casualty Underwriters Society (CPCU), and the National Society of Professional Engineers (NSPE). He offers seminars on negotiation skills for success, persuasive presentations, conflict management, multi-generational communication, and self-leadership.

Before starting his coaching career, Peter worked as a pharmaceutical engineer. His engineering background helps him approach situations from a systems-based perspective, giving him the ability to relate, communicate, and deliver results at all levels of an organization. He helps his training participants quickly acquire the essential management, leadership, self-empowerment, and strategic tools to achieve their goals.

Custom Resource

Accelerate Your Progress with Expert Coaching: The Self-Leadership Guide Coaching Program

This is a proven system to help you get unstuck and start moving in the direction you want.

Get one-on-one support, guidance, and executive coaching around your career goals and dreams. Programs range from one to three sessions a month, over the phone or in person, with an experienced and certified self-leadership guide.

Sometimes coaching is the only way to eliminate procrastination, doubt, and the feeling of being stuck. Start moving towards a career you love today. Call to schedule a free fifteen-minute evaluation and strategy session with one of our expert coaches.

The Self-Leadership Guide Coaching Program will help you implement the strategies and insights you have learned in this book.

Call or Email Today for your Free Fifteen-Minute Evaluation and Strategy Session.

(408) 647-6146
StrategySession@SelfLeadershipGuide.com

Custom Resource

Live Training In Your Organization

1-hour Keynote to One Full Day Workshop: Conducted in Person by Peter Khoury

Now you and your key people can get practical, live and experiential training on Self-Leadership and its application in your organization. Ideal for in-house meetings, conferences, breakout sessions, corporate retreats, etc.

> For more information on our organizational trainings please call, email, or visit us on the web today.
>
> (408) 647-6146
> info@SelfLeadershipGuide.com
> www.SelfLeadershipGuide.com

Extra Worksheets

Your Career Code

GENERAL CRITERIA	SMART CODE GOALS

JOB REQUIREMENTS FOR (EMPLOYEE NAME	PROJECTS, ACTIVITIES, TASKS	SMART GOALS
1.		
2.		
3.		
4.		
5.		
6.